S0-DUW-471

RECEIVED

JAN 24 2020

BROADVIEW LIBRARY

THIS IS NO LONGER THE PROPERTY
OF THE SEATTLE PUBLIC LIBRARY

Lets Look at
Trucks and
Tractors

John Allan

HUNGRY
TOMATO™

MINNEAPOLIS

Thanks to the creative team:
Editor: Tim Harris
Design: Perfect Bound Ltd

Original edition copyright 2019 by Hungry Tomato Ltd.
Copyright © 2019 by Lerner Publishing Group, Inc.

Hungry Tomato® is a trademark of
Lerner Publishing Group

All rights reserved. International copyright secured.
No part of this book may be reproduced, stored in
a retrieval system, or transmitted in any form or by
any means—electronic, mechanical, photocopying,
recording, or otherwise—without the prior written
permission of Lerner Publishing Group, Inc.,
except for the inclusion of brief quotations in an
acknowledged review.

Hungry Tomato®
A division of Lerner Publishing Group, Inc.
241 First Avenue North
Minneapolis, MN 55401 USA

For reading levels and more information,
look up this title at www.lernerbooks.com.

Main body text set in Fibra One Alt.

Library of Congress Cataloging-in-Publication Data

Names: Allan, John, 1961- author.
Title: Let's look at trucks and tractors / John Allan.
Description: Minneapolis, MN : Hungry Tomato, a
division of Lerner Publishing Group, Inc., [2019] |
Series: Mini mechanic | Includes bibliographical
references and index. | Audience: Age 6-9. | Audience:
Grades K to 3. | Identifiers: LCCN 2018049640 (print) |
LCCN 2018059639 (ebook) | ISBN 9781541555303 (eb pdf) |
ISBN 9781541555297 (lb : alk. paper)
Subjects: LCSH: Trucks—Juvenile literature. | Tractors—
Juvenile literature.
Classification: LCC TL230.15 (ebook) | LCC TL230.15 .A45
2019 (print) | DDC 629.224—dc23

LC record available at https://lccn.loc.gov/2018049640

Manufactured in the United States of America
1-45932-42826-1/10/2019

Contents

The Mini Mechanics

Wrenches are used to tighten and loosen nuts.

Nuts and bolts are used on vehicles to hold parts together.

A jack lifts vehicles so we can work underneath them.

We are the mini mechanics. Welcome to our workshop. We work on some amazing vehicles, and these are a few of the tools we use to fix them.

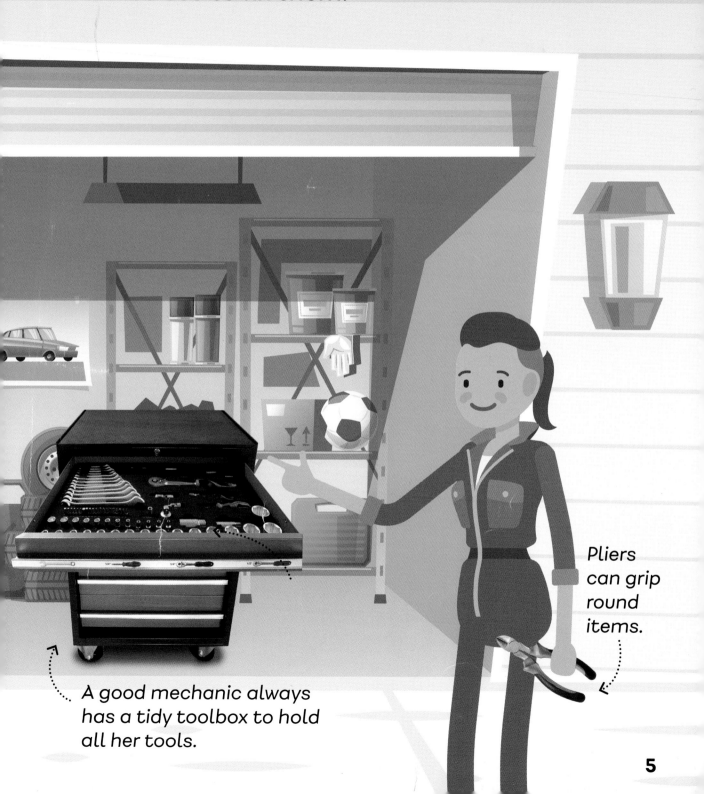

Pliers can grip round items.

A good mechanic always has a tidy toolbox to hold all her tools.

Tractor

Tractors do many jobs on a farm. They work in the sunshine, snow, and rain.

This tractor is lifting a heavy bale of straw.

Tractors have tough, thick wheels to grip in muddy fields.

Tractors have small wheels at the front to help them turn around in small circles.

Tractor and Plow

This tractor is pulling a plow to dig up the earth. Then the farmer can sow seeds into the ground.

This is called a moldboard.
It turns the earth over.

Metal blades cut into
the ground so seeds
can be planted.

Combine Harvester

A combine harvester does two jobs at once. First, it cuts up and gathers the crops. Then it separates the grain from the rest of the plant.

When the tank is full, the grain is emptied into a trailer.

Inside, a spinning drum shakes the grains off the plant.

These spikes push the crops into the combine harvester.

Big Rig Truck

A big rig truck has a powerful engine to pull heavy trailers. It can travel hundreds and thousands of miles to deliver its goods.

Trailers are added to big rigs to haul heavy goods.

Some cabs are so big that the driver can sleep in them.

Big rig trucks use lots of fuel and need big fuel tanks.

Garbage Truck

Garbage trucks collect the trash from our homes. They keep our cities clean.

Garbage trucks pick up trash early in the morning.

These controls operate the machine.

The trash is placed in the back of the truck, where it is crushed.

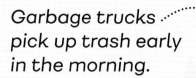

Tanker

This tanker is carrying fuel to run our vehicles or heat our homes. Tankers can carry powders and gases as well as liquids.

Tankers have curved sides because they are stronger than flat ones.

Tankers have signs on them to show what's inside.

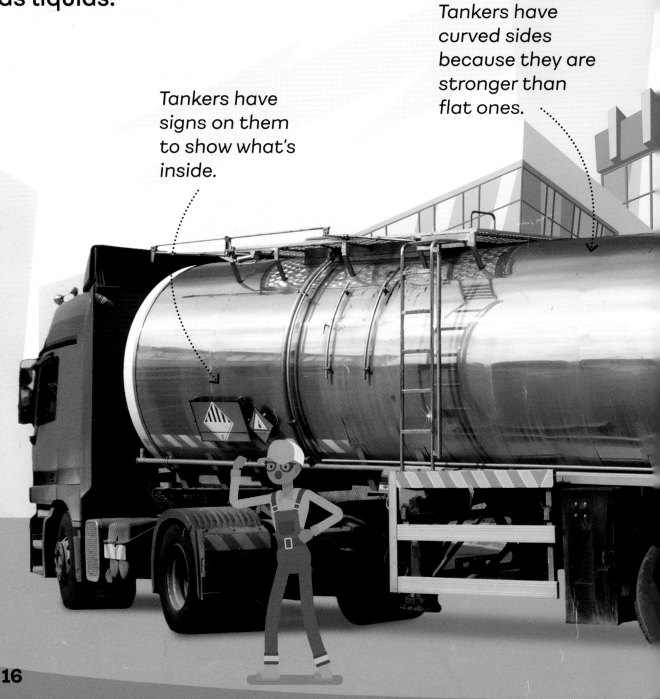

At the gas station, the fuel is poured into big underground tanks using hoses.

Monster Truck

This awesome machine is a pickp truck. It is built to race over bumpy and muddy courses. It is tall so that it can drive over anything in its way.

Each wheel is larger than a person.

This wheel will be put onto a monster truck.

These are giant shock absorbers, which act like cushions as they go over bumps.

Lowboy

A lowboy has a trailer that is low to the ground. This makes it easier to get heavy loads on and off. This one has a large dumper on it.

This dump truck is wider than the trailer. A separate car with flashing lights may drive in front of the lowboy to warn other vehicles.

This trailer has lots of wheels to help carry the heavy load.

This excavating machine is being driven off the trailer.

Tow Truck

A tow truck is used when a vehicle breaks down or has an accident. The tow truck can lift the car out of trouble and then tow it away.

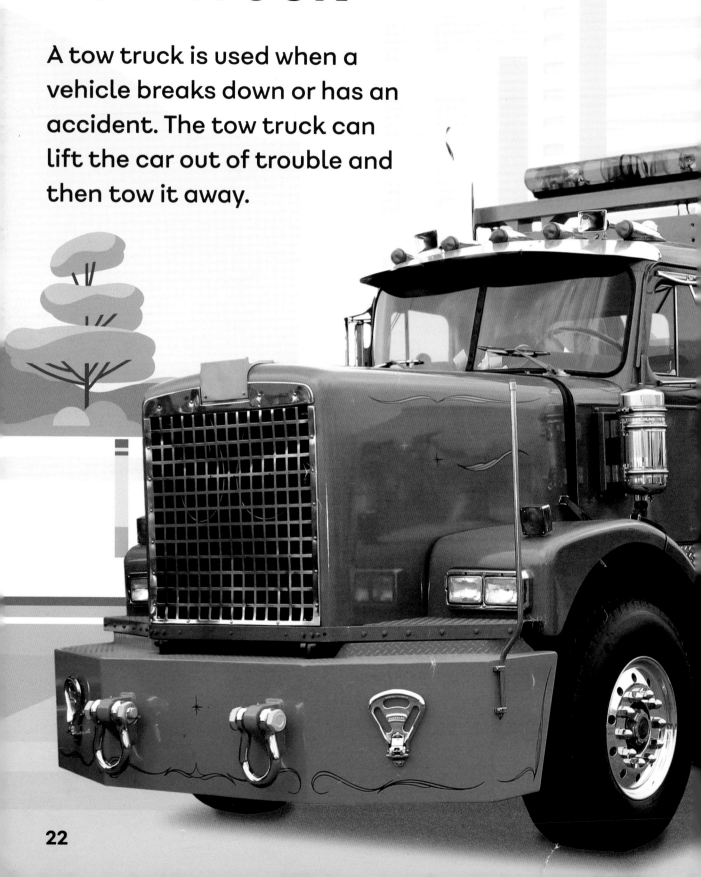

This truck has broken down and is being taken to a garage for repairs.

This cable is made of metal wire and is very strong.

A big hook is used to lift vehicles that need rescuing.

Glossary

blades sharp cutting edges

cabs where drivers sit in vehicles

dumper a truck with a section that lifts to dump its contents

drum a cylindrical container

excavating digging out and removing

sow plant seed

tow to drag or pull something behind

workshop a place where things are made or repaired

Picture Credits
(abbreviations: t = top; b = bottom; m = middle; l = left; r = right; bg = background)

Anastasiia Kozubenko 20bg; Andrew Rybalko (all characters); Archiwiz 4 (wrench); Arthito 5 (pliers); Charles Brutlag 9; David Touchtone 22; DniproDD 1bg, 14bg; Droidworker 2bg, 8bg, 10bg; ezp 6ml; Filip Miletic 5 (toolbox); Fotokostic 9tr; I'm friday 15; Krivosheev Vitaly 10; MadPixel 6bg; Marquisphoto 17tr; MaryDesyv2 18bg; Mastak A 12bg; Mikhail Abramov 4 (jack); Mikhail Martynov 4 (bolts); Nielskliim 15tr; Nigel Jarvis 19; oksana.perkins 13tr; Petr Studen 1; photo-denver 23tr; ProStockStudio 22bg; Reinhard Tiburzy 21; Rihardzz 17; Roman023_photography 21tr; smereka 11tr; timothy passmore 13; Vectorpocket 4bg, 17bg; Vladimir Melnik 19tr.